1112

CR

10623017

SandCastle™

Animal Homes

Home Sweet Tree

Mary Elizabeth Salzmann

CONSULTING EDITOR, DIANE CRAIG, M.A./READING SPECIALIST

ABDO
Publishing Company

visit us at www.abdopublishing.com

Published by ABDO Publishing Company, a division of ABDO, P.O. Box 398166, Minneapolis, Minnesota 55439. Copyright © 2012 by Abdo Consulting Group, Inc. International copyrights reserved in all countries. No part of this book may be reproduced in any form without written permission from the publisher. SandCastle™ is a trademark and logo of ABDO Publishing Company.

Printed in the United States of America, North Mankato, Minnesota
062011
092011

Editor: Katherine Hengel
Content Developer: Nancy Tuminelly
Cover and Interior Design and Production: Anders Hanson, Mighty Media, Inc.
Photo Credits: Shutterstock

Library of Congress Cataloging-in-Publication Data
Salzmann, Mary Elizabeth, 1968-
  Home sweet tree / Mary Elizabeth Salzmann.
     p. cm. -- (Animal homes)
  ISBN 978-1-61714-819-4
  1. Forest animals--Juvenile literature. 2. Animals--Habitations--Juvenile literature. I. Title.
  QL112.S27 2012
  591.56'4--dc22
                          2010053050

SANDCASTLE™ LEVEL: TRANSITIONAL

SandCastle™ books are created by a team of professional educators, reading specialists, and content developers around five essential components—phonemic awareness, phonics, vocabulary, text comprehension, and fluency—to assist young readers as they develop reading skills and strategies and increase their general knowledge. All books are written, reviewed, and leveled for guided reading, early reading intervention, and Accelerated Reader® programs for use in shared, guided, and independent reading and writing activities to support a balanced approach to literacy instruction. The SandCastle™ series has four levels that correspond to early literacy development. The levels are provided to help teachers and parents select appropriate books for young readers.

Emerging Readers
(no flags)

Beginning Readers
(1 flag)

Transitional Readers
(2 flags)

Fluent Readers
(3 flags)

Contents

What Is a Tree?

A tree is a very tall plant. It has a large stem called a trunk.

Trees have branches that grow out of the trunk. Leaves or **needles** grow on the branches.

Animals and Trees

Animals that live in trees are called arboreal animals. Most arboreal animals live in **tropical** forests.

Toucans live in trees.

Toucans live in holes dug into tree trunks.
A toucan will move into a hole made by
another animal.

The emerald tree boa lives in a tree.

At night emerald tree boas hang from low branches. They **grab prey** that passes by on the ground.

Tree frogs live in trees.

Tree frogs have sticky **pads** on their toes. The pads help them **grip** leaves and branches.

The Jackson's chameleon lives in a tree.

Jackson's chameleons are found in mountain forests in Africa. They eat bugs that they catch with their long, sticky tongues.

Howler monkeys live in trees.

Howler monkeys can hold onto tree branches with their long tails. Their calls can be heard up to 3 miles (5 km) away.

Koalas live in trees.

Koalas live in **eucalyptus** trees and eat the leaves. A koala eats 2 to 3 pounds (1 to 1.3 kg) of leaves a day.

Tree squirrels live in trees.

Some tree squirrels live in tree holes. Other tree squirrels build nests out of sticks and leaves.

Could *you*
live in a tree?

Quiz

1. No arboreal animals live in **tropical** forests. *True or false?*

2. Toucans live in holes in tree trunks. *True or false?*

3. Tree frogs do not have sticky **pads** on their toes. *True or false?*

4. Howler monkeys can hold onto tree branches with their tails. *True or false?*

5. Koalas live in **eucalyptus** trees. *True or false?*

Glossary

eucalyptus – an Australian tree that is grown for its oil and wood.

grab – to take hold of something suddenly.

grip – to hold onto.

needle – a thin, pointy leaf on a pine or fir tree.

pad – the bottom of an animal's toe or foot.

prey – an animal that is hunted or caught for food.

tropical – located in one of the hottest areas on earth.